kanaviçe

EASY CROSS STITCH SERIES ④
BORDERS

Maria Diaz

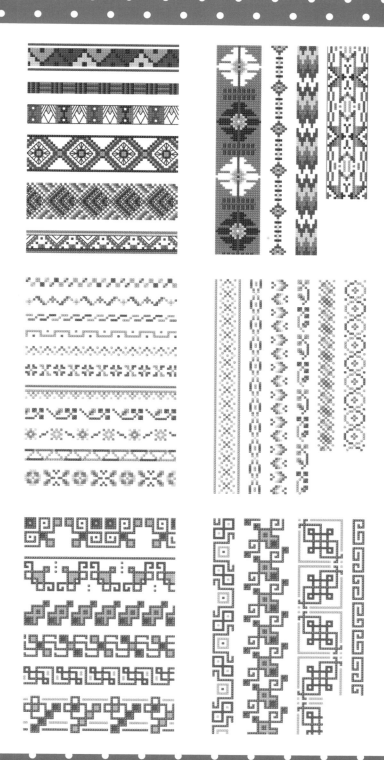

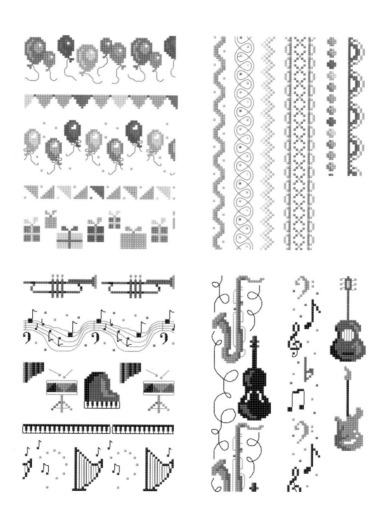

9

Mouliné
Stranded Cotton Art. 117

▣	321
+	725
▢	892
I	947
3	995
✕	3708
—	3819

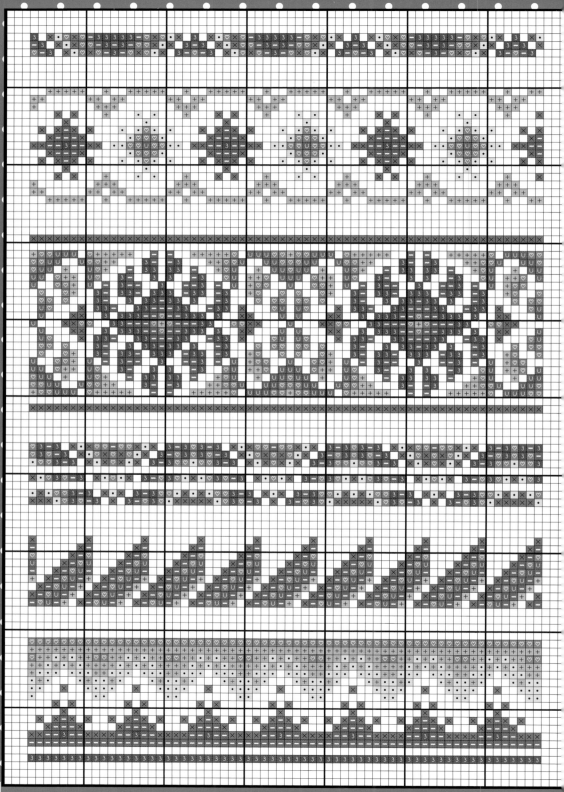

Mouliné
Stranded Cotton Art. 117

U		321
•		727
3		791
♡		947
+		972
−		995
✕		3846

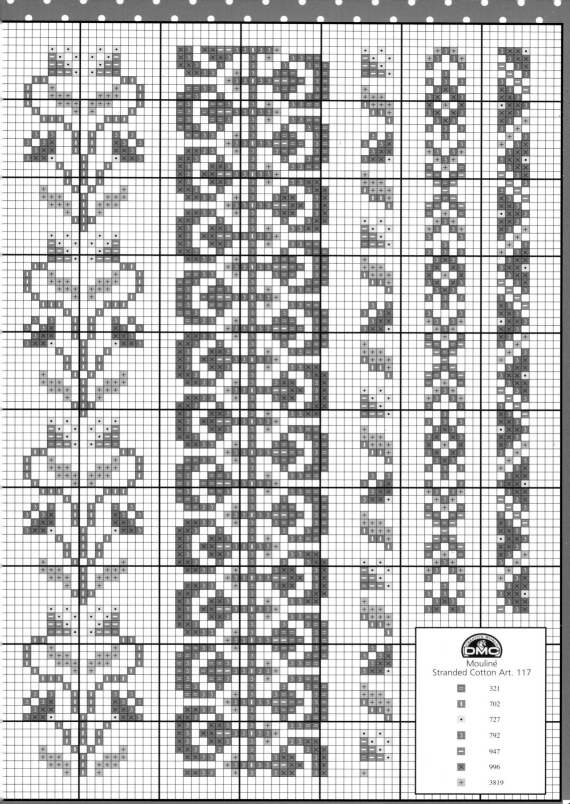

Mouliné
Stranded Cotton Art. 117

⊟	321
⫾	702
•	727
3	792
⊟	947
✕	996
+	3819

15

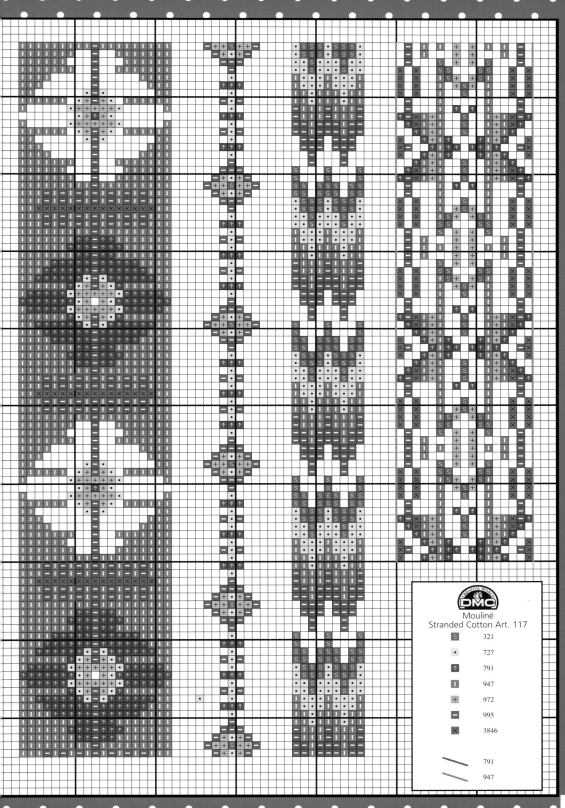

DMC
Mouliné
Stranded Cotton Art. 117

S	321
•	727
↑	791
I	947
+	972
−	995
✕	3846

/	791
/	947

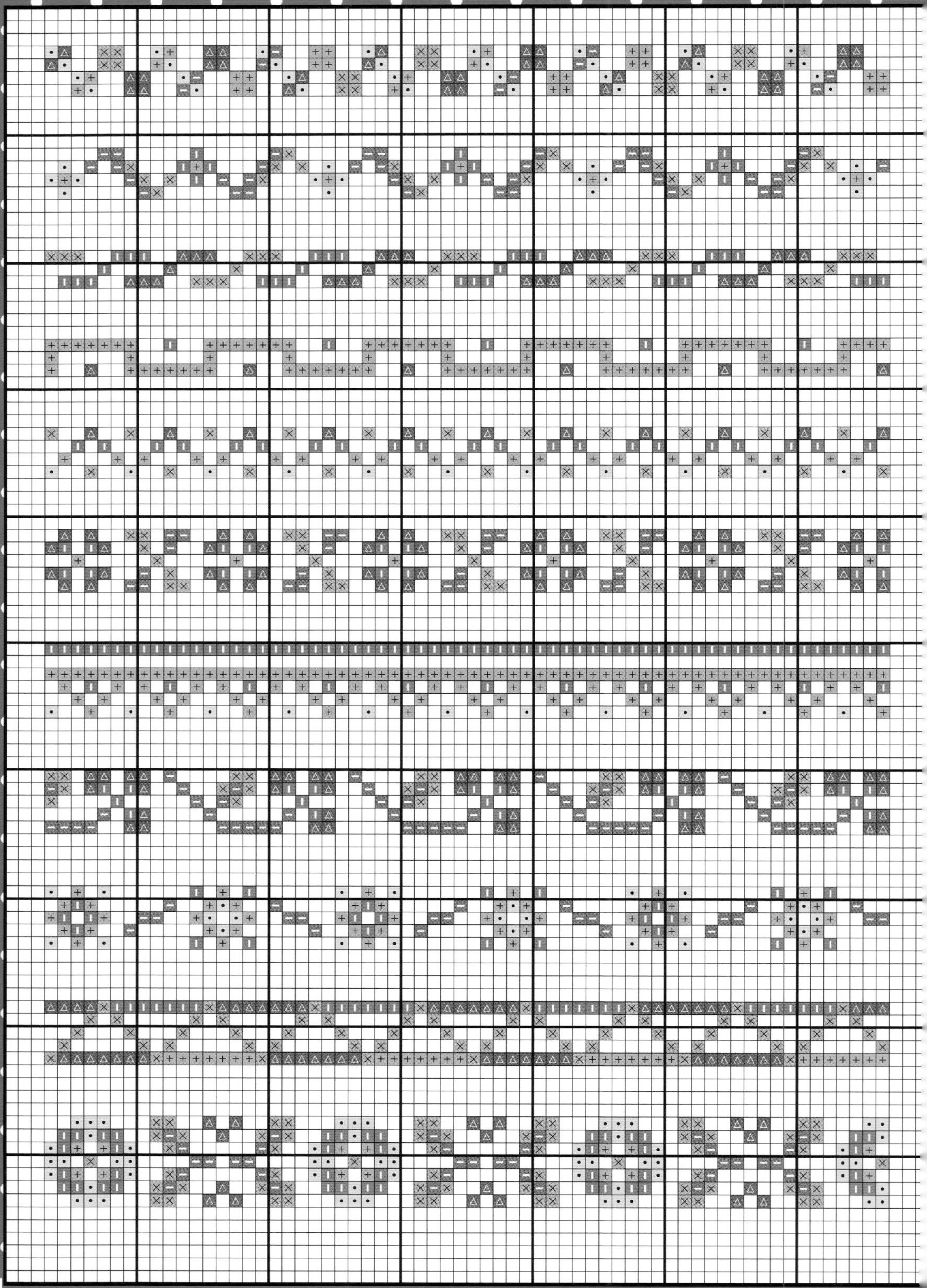

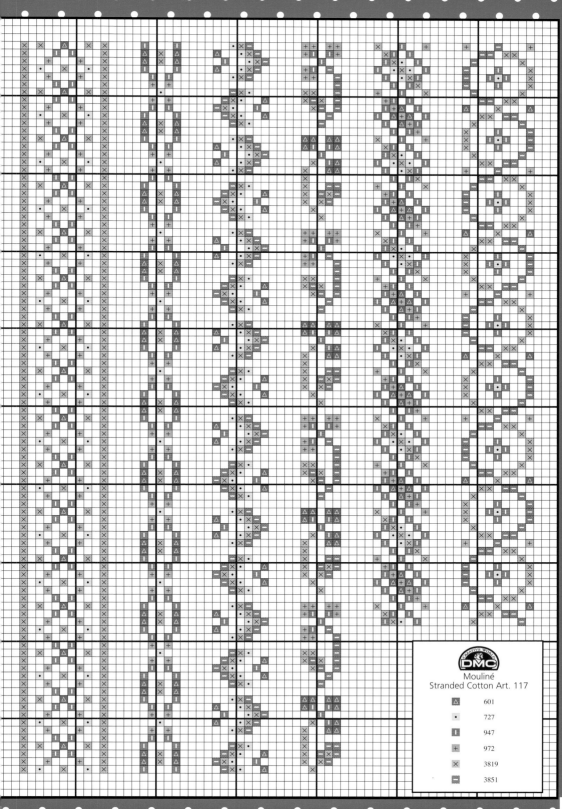

DMC
Mouliné
Stranded Cotton Art. 117

△	601
•	727
I	947
+	972
×	3819
▬	3851

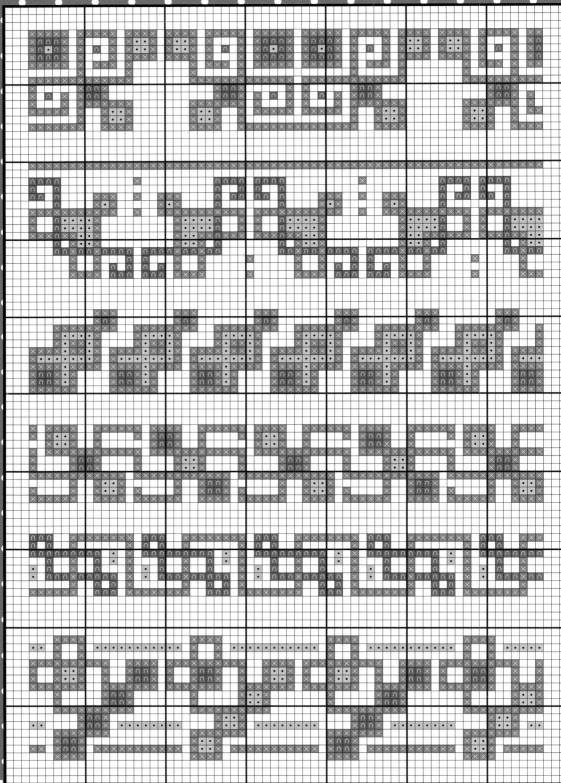

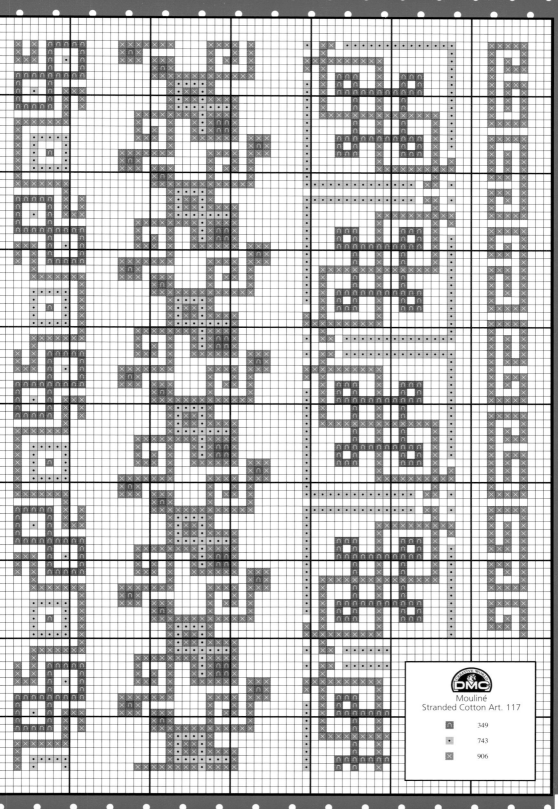

Mouliné
Stranded Cotton Art. 117

∩	349
•	743
✕	906

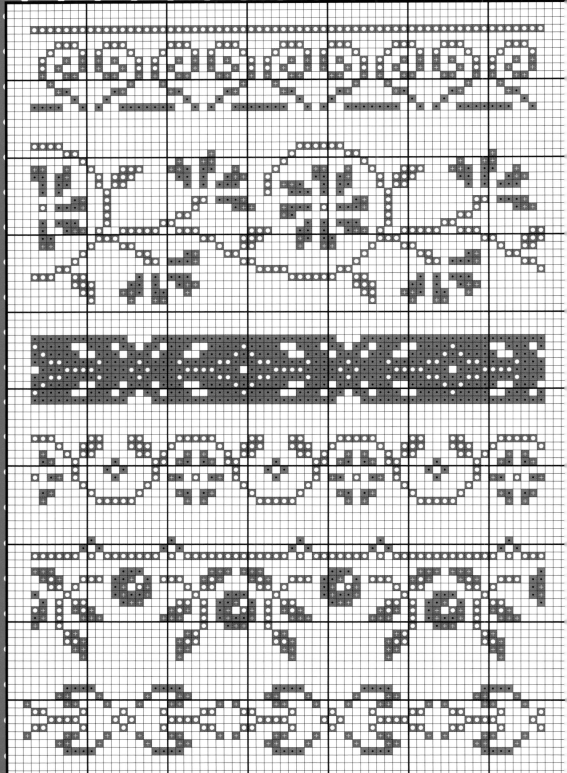

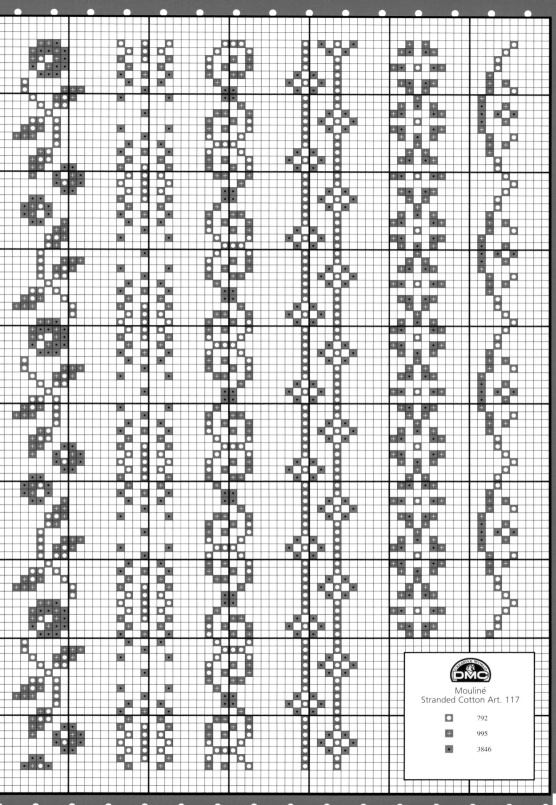

Mouliné
Stranded Cotton Art. 117

▢	792
✚	995
•	3846

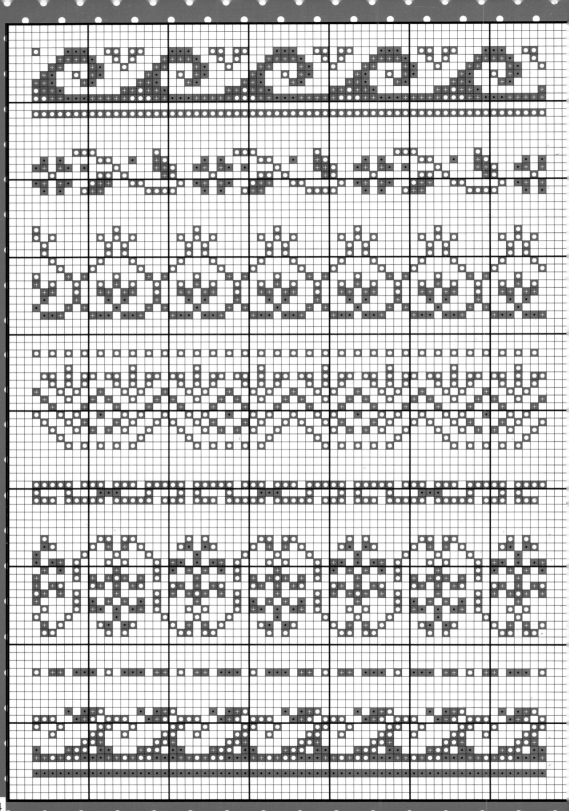

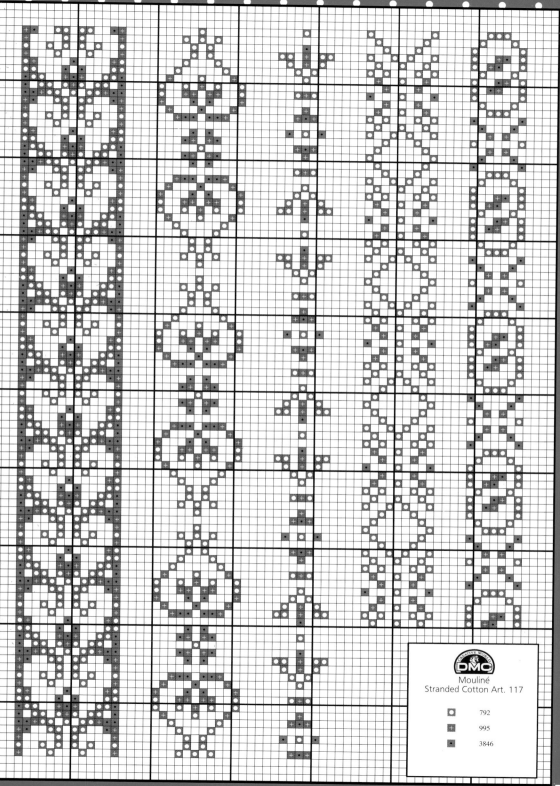

Mouliné
Stranded Cotton Art. 117

⊡	792
✛	995
▪	3846

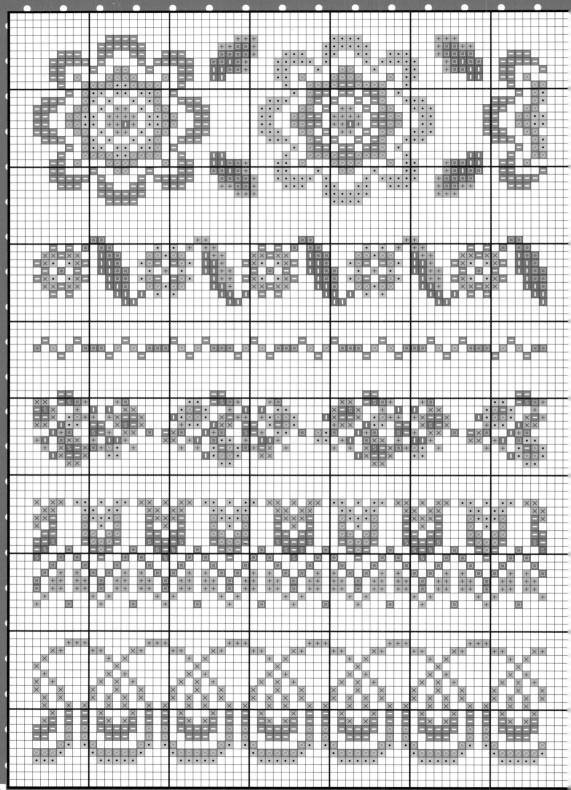

Mouliné
Stranded Cotton Art. 117

▣	702
S	718
·	725
◎	740
▬	956
×	957
▐	958
+	3819

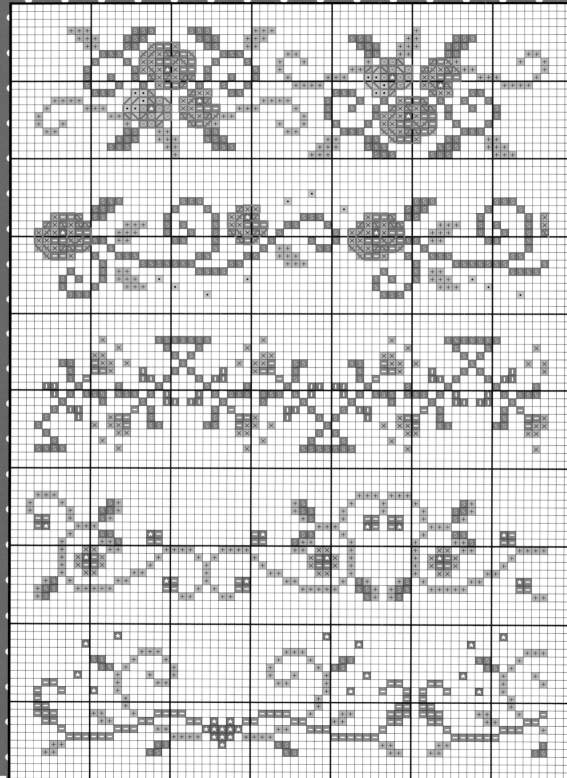

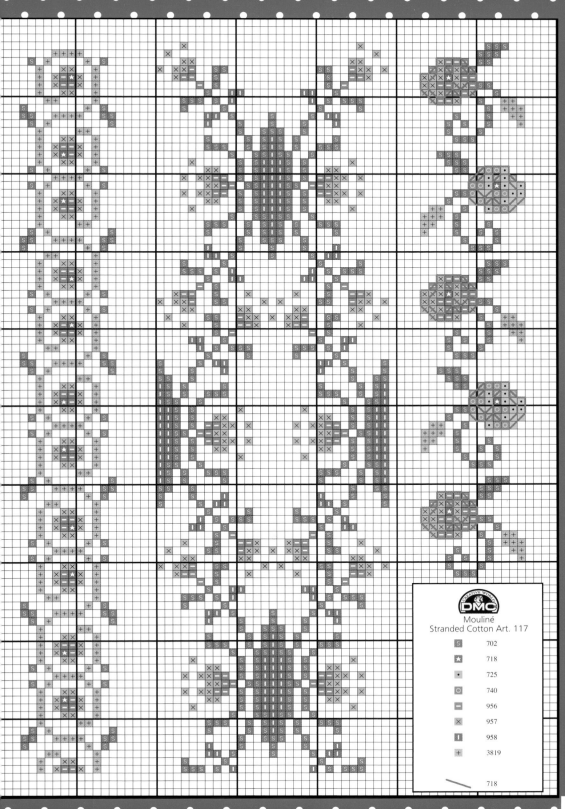

DMC

Mouliné
Stranded Cotton Art. 117

S	702
★	718
•	725
○	740
–	956
✕	957
I	958
+	3819

718

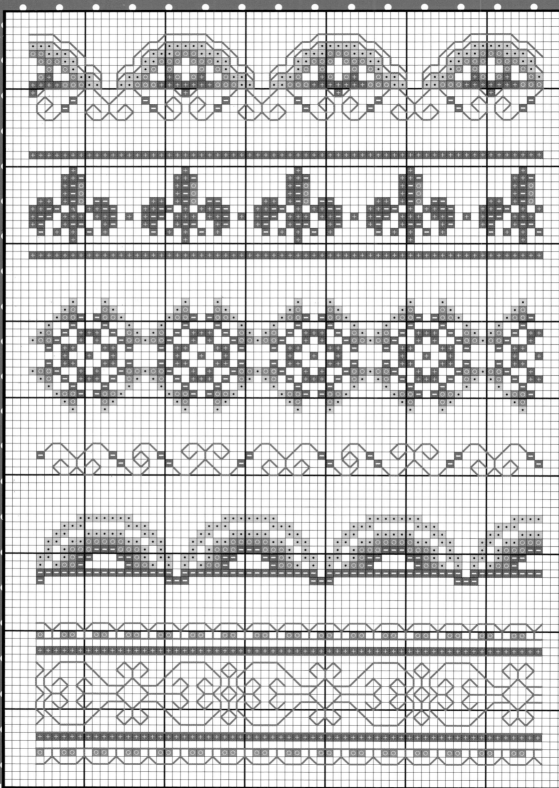

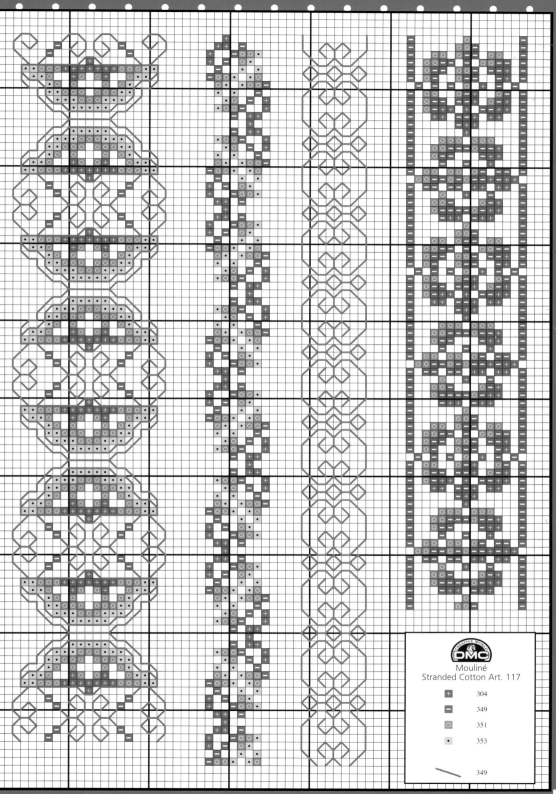

Mouliné
Stranded Cotton Art. 117

+	304
–	349
⊙	351
•	353
/	349

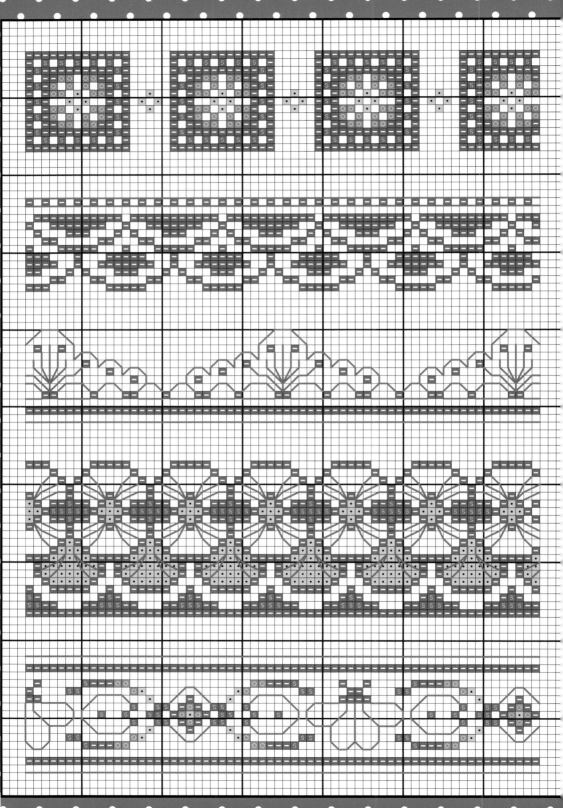

DMC
Mouliné
Stranded Cotton Art. 117

S	304
▬	349
⊙	351
•	353
╱	349

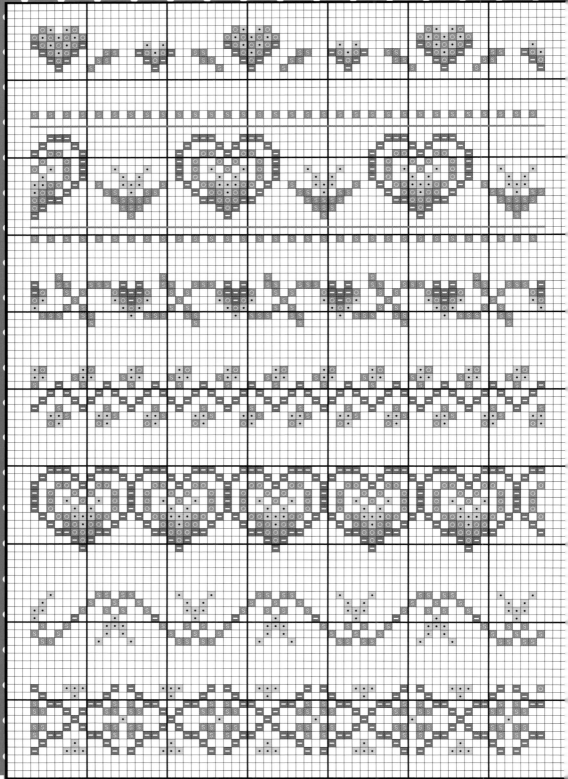

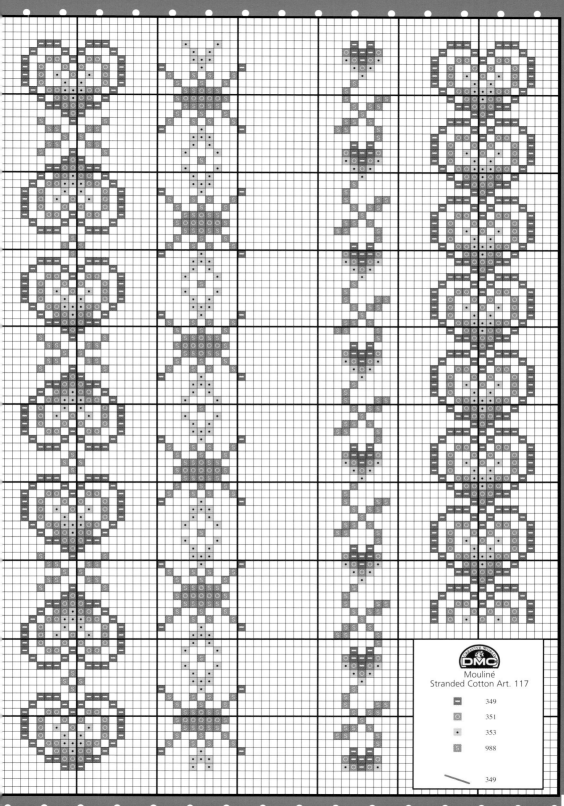

Mouliné
Stranded Cotton Art. 117

▬	349
◎	351
•	353
S	988
╱	349

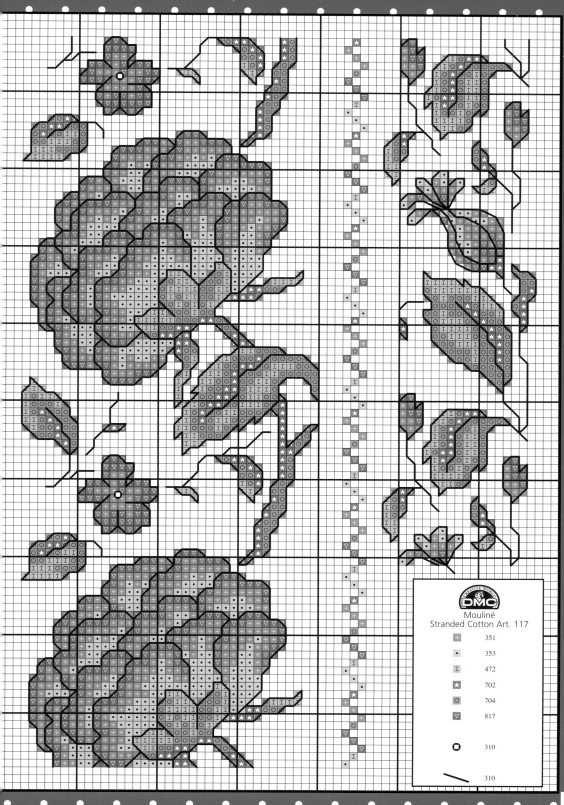

DMC
CREATIVE WORLD
Mouliné
Stranded Cotton Art. 117

Symbol	Number
+	351
•	353
I	472
★	702
◎	704
▽	817
○	310
╱	310

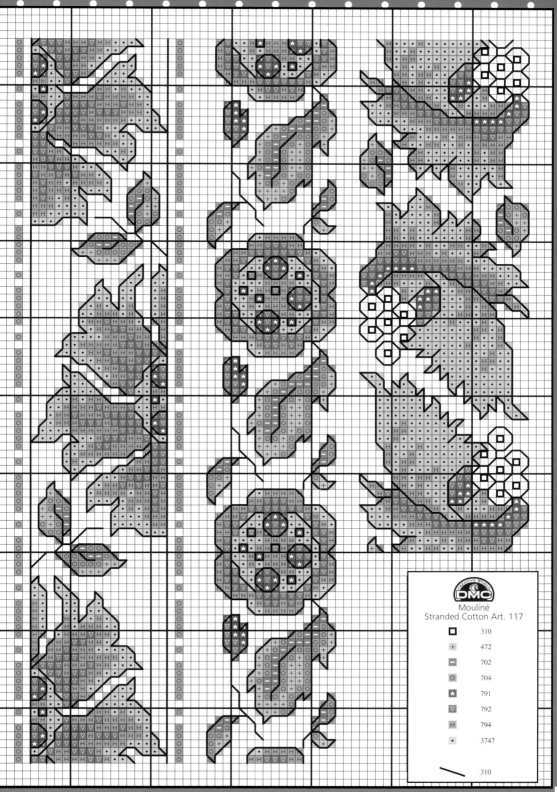

DMC
Creative World
Mouliné
Stranded Cotton Art. 117

■	310
+	472
▬	702
◉	704
★	791
▽	792
H	794
•	3747
╱	310

DMC
Mouliné
Stranded Cotton Art. 117

H	157
O	704
–	701
★	791
▽	793
/	791

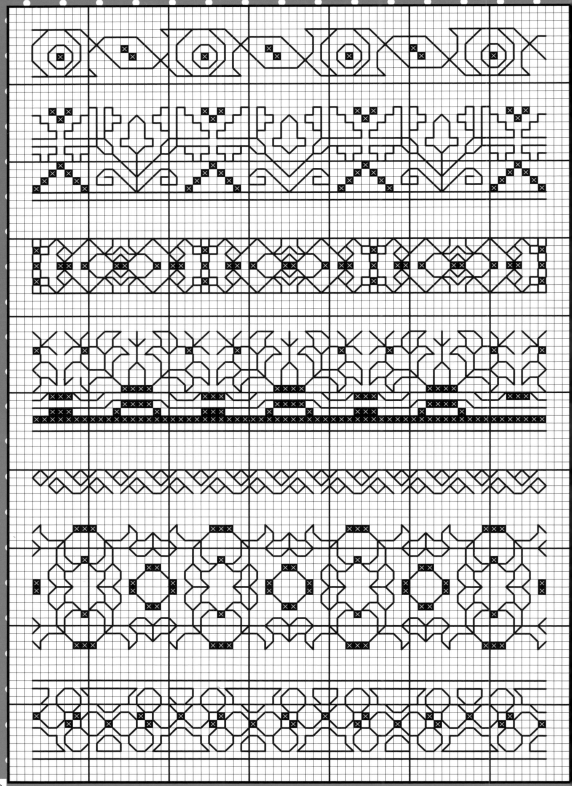

DMC
CREATIVE WORLD
Mouliné
Stranded Cotton Art. 117

☒ 310

／ 310

43

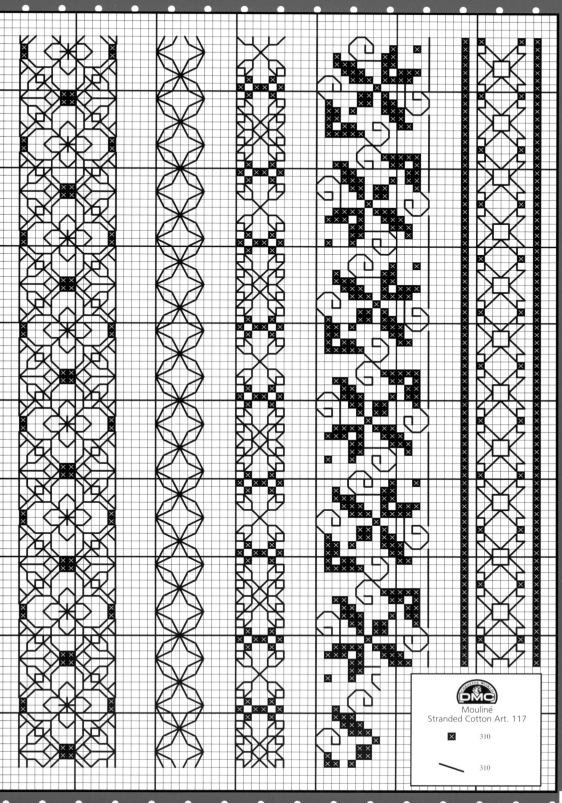

Mouliné
Stranded Cotton Art. 117

☒	310
╱	310

45

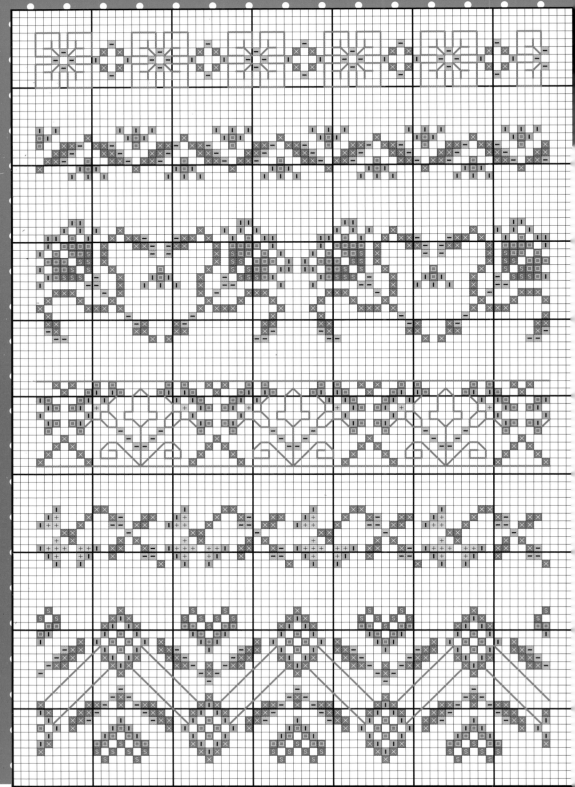

DMC
Mouliné
Stranded Cotton Art. 117

S	321
+	726
I	741
□	892
−	3819
⊠	3850
	3850

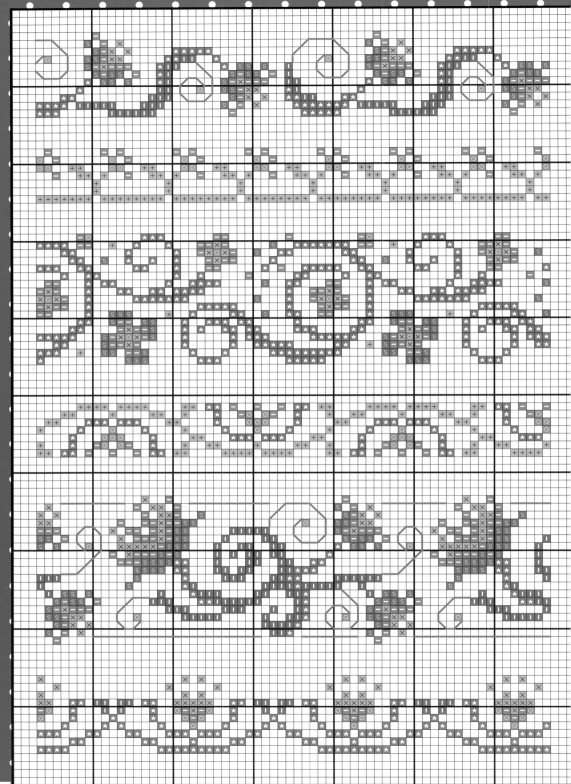

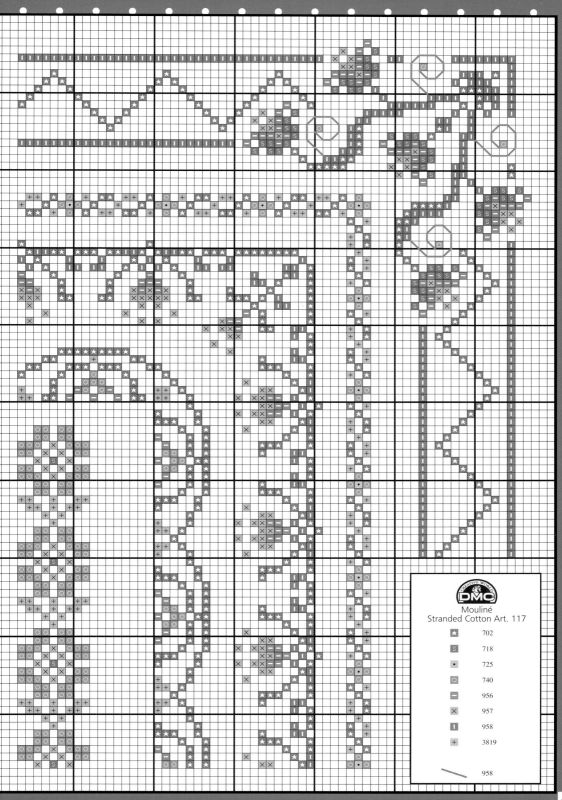

Mouliné
Stranded Cotton Art. 117

★	702
S	718
·	725
○	740
—	956
✕	957
I	958
+	3819
╱	958

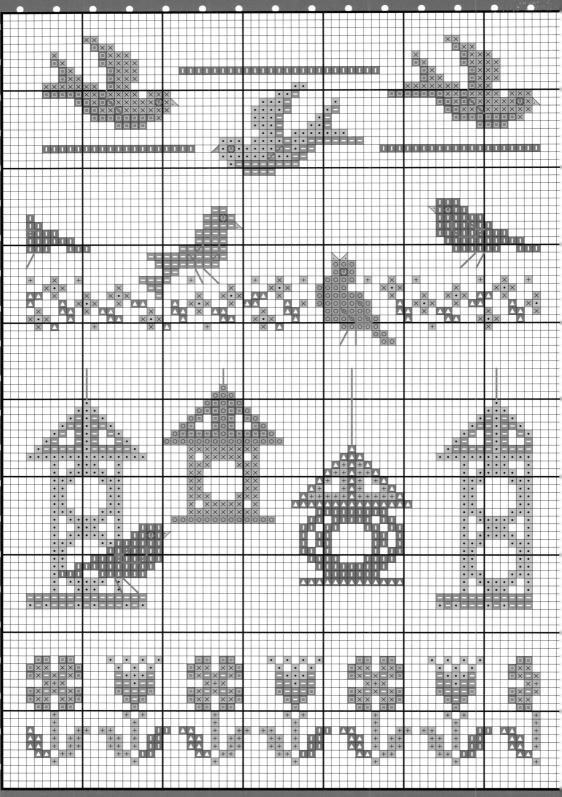

DMC
Mouliné
Stranded Cotton Art. 117

◙	209	
▲	702	
•	725	
▬	740	
▣	956	
✕	957	
▮	958	
+	3819	
╱	3837	
∪	3837	

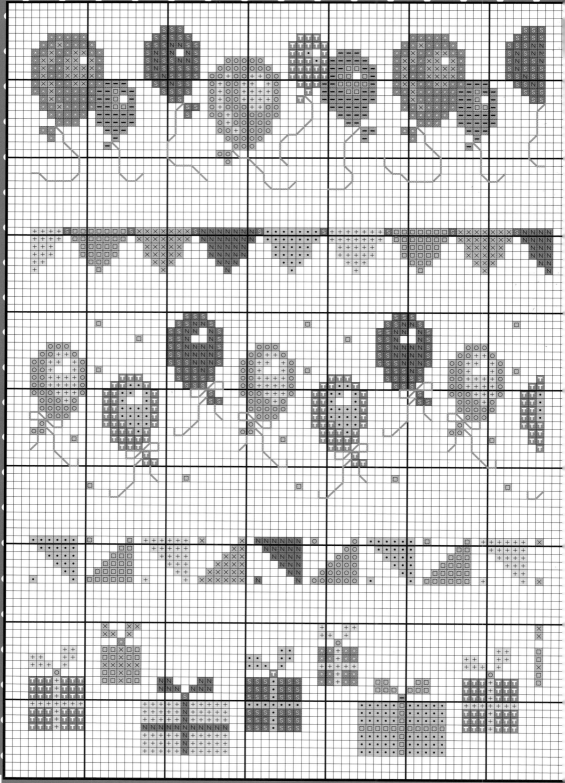

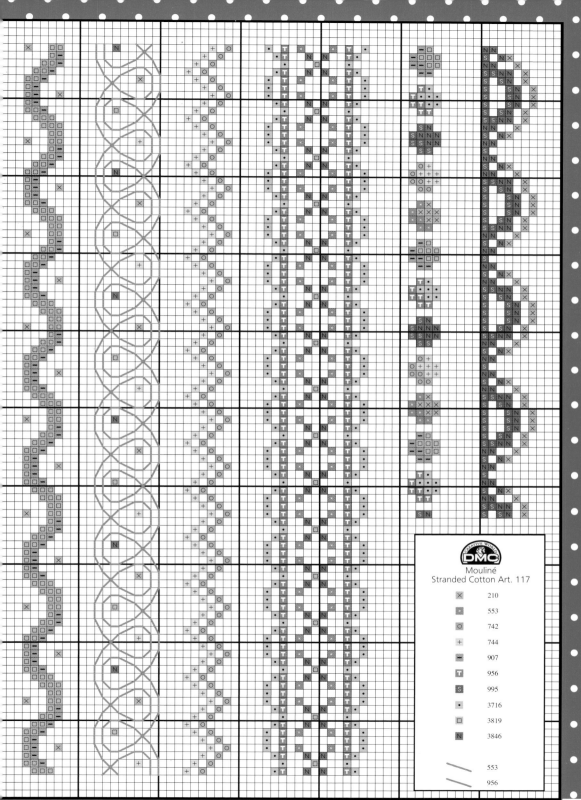

DMC
Mouliné
Stranded Cotton Art. 117

Symbol	Number
✕	210
⊡	553
○	742
+	744
−	907
T	956
S	995
•	3716
□	3819
N	3846

| | 553 |
| | 956 |

53

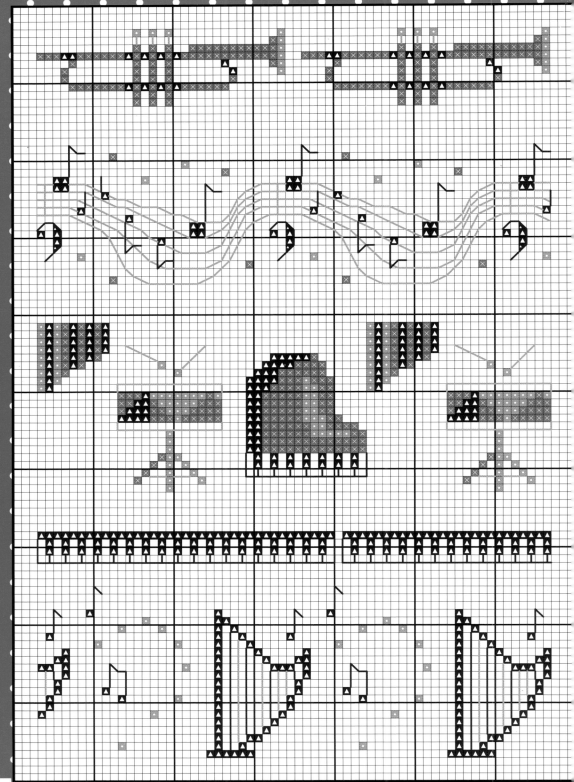

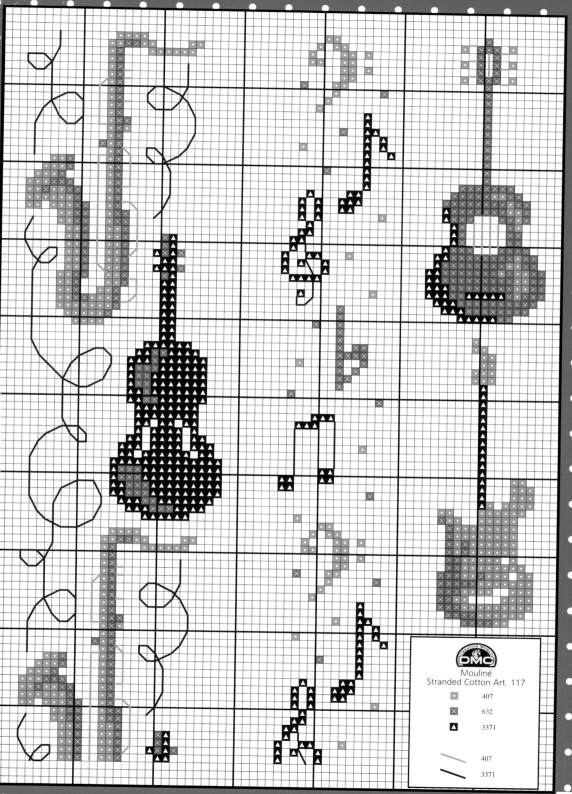

Mouliné
Stranded Cotton Art. 117

⊡	407
⊠	632
▲	3371

───	407
───	3371